WAS IST LERNEN AN STATIONEN?

Beim Lernen an Stationen handelt es sich um eine Form selbstständigen Arbeitens, bei der

- ☐ unterschiedliche Lernvoraussetzungen,
- ☐ unterschiedliche Zugänge und Betrachtungsweisen,
- ☐ unterschiedliches Lern- und Arbeitstempo
- ☐ und häufig fächerübergreifendes Arbeiten

berücksichtigt werden.

Grundidee

Den Schülerinnen und Schülern werden Arbeitsstationen zur individuellen Bearbeitung angeboten, an welchen sie selbstständig, in beliebiger Abfolge und meist auch in frei gewählter Sozialform entsprechend ihren Möglichkeiten und Fähigkeiten arbeiten. Damit soll ihnen optimales Lernen und Üben ermöglicht werden.

Herkunft und Entwicklung

Die Idee des Lernens an Stationen, auch Lernzirkel genannt, kommt ursprünglich aus dem Sportbereich.
Das „circuit training", von Morgan und Adamson 1952 in England entwickelt, stellt den Sportlern unterschiedliche Übungsstationen zur Verfügung, die sie der Reihe nach oder in freier Auswahl durchlaufen.
Eine Übertragung dieser Lernform auf Unterrichtsinhalte in verschiedenen Fächern wurde zunächst an der Schallenbergschule in Aidlingen/Baden-Württemberg, später am Seminar für schulpraktische Ausbildung in Sindelfingen und seit etwa 1980 an vielen Schulen aufgegriffen und stetig weiterentwickelt.
Der Herausgeber und die Autoren stellen die Ergebnisse ihrer eigenen praktischen Arbeit und Erfahrung in dieser Reihe vor und bieten ihre Materialien als Grundlage für den direkten Einsatz oder als Grundlage für eine Anpassung an eigene Bedürfnisse an.

Zielrichtungen

Das Lernen an Stationen kann unterschiedliche Ziele verfolgen:

- ☐ optimales Üben ermöglichen durch ein breites Angebot, das die verschiedenen Lerneingangskanäle, allgemeine Übungsgesetze, unterschiedliche Aufgabenarten, Schwierigkeiten und Hilfestellungen berücksichtigt,
- ☐ vertiefendes Bearbeiten eines Inhalts beziehungsweise eines Themengebietes, indem Schülerinnen und Schüler nach zuvor gestalteter Übersicht oder Einführung die Inhalte auf ihre Art, mit ihren Möglichkeiten und in ihrem individuellen Tempo auf unterschiedlichen Ebenen selbstständig bearbeiten,
- ☐ selbstständiges Erarbeiten von Themengebieten, indem die Schülerinnen und Schüler durch angemessene Arbeitsangebote Sachverhalte hinterfragen, erforschen, erfahren, gestalten usw.,
- ☐ Angebote aus Schulbüchern oder Medien unter ganzheitlicher Betrachtungsweise aufarbeiten, indem die Schülerinnen und Schüler Aufgabenstellungen zu Teilgebieten mit unterschiedlicher Betrachtungsweise und auf unterschiedlichen Ebenen fächerübergreifend bearbeiten.

Organisation

Die einzelnen Arbeitsaufträge geben den Schülerinnen und Schülern klare oder offene Aufgabenstellungen mit eindeutigen Anweisungen. Die Angebote werden im Klassenzimmer zur Verfügung gestellt, indem der Arbeitsauftrag durch Aushängen oder Auslegen bereitgestellt wird. Dazu bietet sich zum Schutz das Verpacken in Prospekthüllen an.
Als Ort zum Aushängen eignen sich alle Wand- und zum Teil auch die Fensterflächen. Pinn-Nadeln oder Nägel (Nagelleisten) erleichtern das Aufhängen und Abnehmen. Beim Auslegen der Arbeitsangebote bzw. -aufträge helfen Ablagekörbe, Ordnung zu halten.
Das Bereitstellen außerhalb der Schülerarbeitstische (also auf Fensterbänken, Nebentischen oder durch Aufhängen) erübrigt das tägliche Aufbauen und Wiederabräumen, stellt also eine große zeitliche und organisatorische Erleichterung dar. Falls im „Fachlehrerbetrieb" der ständige Abbau nötig ist, sind ineinander stapelbare Ablagekörbe, in denen die Aufträge verbleiben, sehr hilfreich.
Die Kennzeichnung der einzelnen Stationen durch Ziffern, Buchstaben oder Symbole hilft den Schülerinnen und Schülern bei der Orientierung. Durch bewusste Verwendung dieser Ordnungsangebote kann die Struktur des Themengebietes oder eine andere Struktur (z. B. Arbeitsform o. Ä.) gleichzeitig verdeutlicht werden.

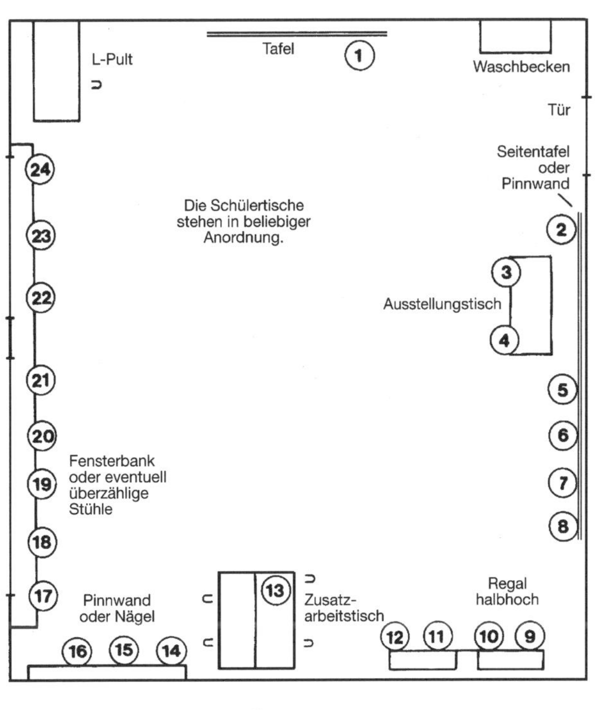

Eine Fortschrittsliste bzw. ein Laufzettel gibt Schülerinnen und Schülern wie den Lehrkräften jederzeit eine Rückmeldung über den derzeitigen Bearbeitungsstand und dient der Übersicht.

Auswahlangebote

Den Schülerinnen und Schülern ist sinnvollerweise ein Auswahlangebot zu ermöglichen; Minimalanforderungen können von der Lehrerin oder dem Lehrer definiert werden. Als Orientierungshilfe finden Sie dazu in den Hinweisen zu diesem Themenheft weitere Angaben.

Sonstige Tipps

Organisatorische Bedingungen und Festlegungen sind möglichst an der konkreten Situation und erst beim tatsächlichen Bedarf zu klären und zu regeln. Ist die Klassenstärke größer als die Anzahl der zur Verfügung stehenden Arbeitsstationen, können Sie die einzelnen Arbeitsaufträge mehrfach anfertigen. Weitere Hinweise zur Organisation, zu den Inhalten und zum Lernen an Stationen allgemein finden Sie im Einführungsband zu dieser Reihe, der unter dem Titel *Schülergerechtes Arbeiten in der Sekundarstufe I: Lernen an Stationen* beim Cornelsen Verlag Scriptor (ISBN 3-589-21117-2) erschienen ist.

Roland Bauer (Herausgeber)

ALLGEMEINE HINWEISE ZU DIESEM THEMENHEFT

Die vorliegenden Stationen machen die Schüler zum einen mit dem Thema Schottland vertraut, stellen aber gleichzeitig auch Übungsmaterial zu den englischen Zeiten dar.

Mit Texten zu Themenbereichen, die den altersspezifischen Interessen der Schüler entgegenkommen oder die ihnen zumindest in Ansätzen bekannt sind, erhalten sie landeskundliche Informationen.

Anhand dieser Inhalte werden dann die englischen Zeiten *will-* und *going to-future, simple present, present progressive, present perfect, simple past* und *past perfect* geübt.
Daraus ergibt sich folgende Matrix, die es erlaubt, auch einzelne Inhaltsbereiche oder Zeiten herauszugreifen:

	Text	**Positive Statements**	**Negative Statements**	**Questions**	**Translation**	**Text-production**
A Future	1: Castles and ghosts	2: Planning the GRAND TOUR of Scotland	3: A letter from Castle Hotel	4: Questions about castles and ghosts		5: A night in an old castle
B Simple Present	1: Scottish sports	2: Keep fit – daily sports	3: Scottish sports are different	4: Finding a sporting partner		5: A sporting man
C Present Progressive	1: The Highland Games	2: What are they doing at the Highland Games?	3: What are the "heavies" doing?	(see: C3 "variation")	4: Help the Germans to understand the explanations	5: A TV-report about the Braemar Highland Games
D Present Perfect	1: Kilts and clans	2: Meeting the Frazer Clan	3: True or false? Facts about Scotland		4: At a woollen mill	5: How to wear a "big" kilt
E Simple Past	1: Scottish inventions	2: What did the inventors do?	3: Are these the right inventions?	4: Talking about an inventor		5: A story about the invention of the pedal-bike
F Past Perfect	1: Loch Ness and Nessie	2: The Loch Ness Monster Exhibition		3: The Nessie game	4: Nessie is joking	5: A postcard from Loch Ness

Zu den einzelnen Zeiten werden zunächst grammatikalische Besonderheiten dieser Zeit geübt (z. B. Unterscheidung nach since und for im present perfect), weiterhin Verneinungen, Fragebildungen, Übersetzungen/Verständnis und Textproduktion.
Die Stationen berücksichtigen die verschiedenen Lerntypen. Sie lassen die unterschiedlichsten Sozialformen (Einzel-, Partner- und Gruppenarbeit) zu und berücksichtigen unterschiedliche Methoden und Arbeitsformen.

Zur besseren Orientierung für die Schüler, aber auch für die Lehrkraft, empfiehlt es sich, die einzelnen Lernbereiche (A–F) jeweils auf gleichfarbiges Papier zu kopieren.
Die Lösungsblätter sollten getrennt von den Aufgabenblättern den Schülern zur Verfügung gestellt werden. Dazu können sie z. B. auf die Rückseite der Klapptafel geklebt werden oder als Nachschlagemappe auf dem Lehrerpult ausliegen.

MATERIALLISTE UND ANMERKUNGEN

E: Scottish inventions

F: Loch Ness and Nessie

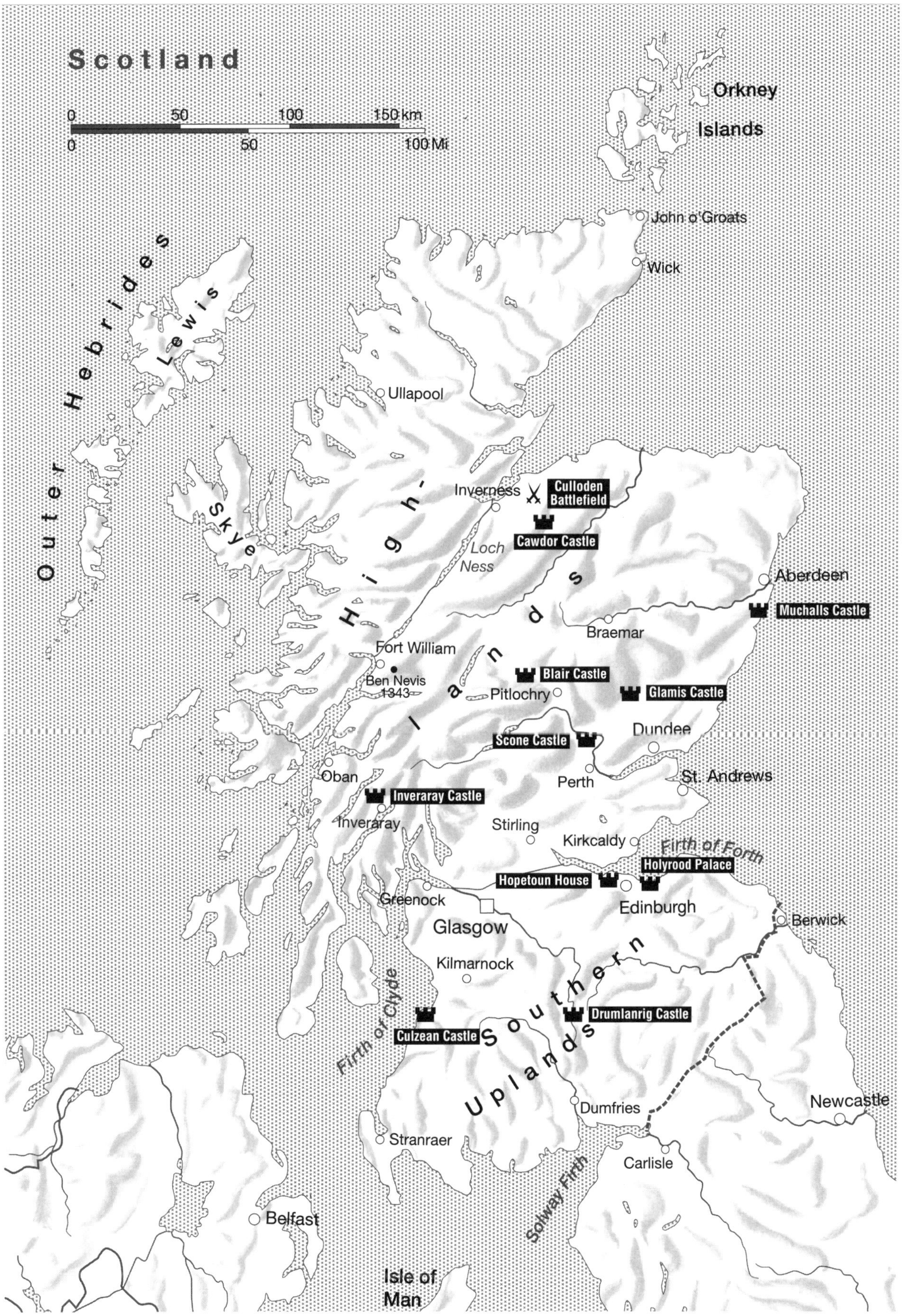
Scotland
0 50 100 150 km
0 50 100 Mi
Orkney Islands
John o'Groats
Wick
Outer Hebrides
Lewis
Ullapool
Skye
Highlands
Inverness
Culloden Battlefield
Cawdor Castle
Loch Ness
Aberdeen
Muchalls Castle
Braemar
Fort William
Ben Nevis 1343
Blair Castle
Pitlochry
Glamis Castle
Dundee
Scone Castle
Oban
Perth
St. Andrews
Inveraray Castle
Inveraray
Stirling
Kirkcaldy
Firth of Forth
Holyrood Palace
Hopetoun House
Edinburgh
Greenock
Glasgow
Berwick
Kilmarnock
Southern Uplands
Firth of Clyde
Drumlanrig Castle
Culzean Castle
Newcastle
Dumfries
Stranraer
Carlisle
Solway Firth
Belfast
Isle of Man

LAUFZETTEL VON: ....

Die folgenden Stationen habe ich schon geschafft:

CASTLES AND GHOSTS

- Read the text “Castles and Ghosts”.
- Look up any new words in your dictionary. Write down the new words in your exercise book.
- Take the map of Scotland and try to find Braemar, Blair Castle, Pitlochry, Edinburgh, Aberdeen and Muchalls Castle.

Material: dictionary, exercise-book, map of Scotland

If you are looking for historic Scotland there will be places where you know you’ve found it: Those places are the castles.
Many of them were built during medieval times and can tell interesting stories about famous people. The owners are usually very proud of their castles – especially if a king or a queen visited them. So they open their castles for visitors and tell them about the popularity of the building and the famous persons who visited it. Some owners redecorated their castle and use it as a hotel now. It is very expensive to run a castle and those are two ways to earn money with these big old buildings.
A very famous castle is Balmoral Castle near Braemar in the Dee Valley. It’s the summer residence of the Royals and every year from August to September the Royal Family leaves London to stay in the Dee Valley. The Queen has to stay in Scotland for at least three months a year by order of the Treaty of Union of the year 1707. Otherwise she would lose her status as Queen of Scotland. Then the tourists try to get a view of the gardens and want to see the Royal Family.
Blair Castle near Pitlochry is around 700 years old. Queen Victoria visited the castle in 1844 and allowed the Dukes to have a private army. It is called “the Atholl Highlanders” and it’s the only private army in Scotland that is still in existence today.
At the end of the Royal Mile in Edinburgh you can find Holyrood Palace, a castle known today as Queen Elizabeth II’s official residence. It is used for banquets whenever the Queen visits the palace. A chamber in James V Tower is associated with Mary, Queen of Scotland who saw the murder of her secretary there. In 1745 Bonnie Prince Charlie (Charles Edward Stuart) held court at Holyrood Palace.
Scottish castles are also famous for their ghosts. It is said that some dead people can’t find peace and walk through the castles as ghosts. The following story is told about the Lady of Muchalls Castle, south of Aberdeen: There is a passage under the castle that leads to a cave on the seashore. Lady Muchalls’ lover was a smuggler. One day she saw her lover’s boat sailing into the cave. At once she ran through the secret passage to meet him but she slipped and fell into the water. By the time he had landed she was drowned. Nowadays she wanders the walls and you can hear a scrubbing noise as she brushes her hair for her lover.
Almost every castle has its own ghost story, telling the visitors that the ghost will appear at midnight. Have you ever heard about a Scottish ghost story?

PLANNING THE GRAND TOUR OF SCOTLAND

Imagine: You want to go to Scotland in your next summer holidays. You have heard about "The GRAND TOUR" of Scotland which takes you to different castles. There are a lot of castles in Scotland. Look at the map.

- Plan your personal Castle Tour and write it down.
  You might start like this: *"First we will visit ..., then we will ..."*
- You have decided to write to the tourist information centre in Glasgow.
  Fill in the *going to-future* or the *will-future*!
  - You may type your letter on the computer.
    Otherwise you can copy it into your exercise book.
  - Compare your solution with the answer key.

Greater Glasgow Tourist Board
35-39 St Vincent Place,
Glasgow G1, UK

_________, ___________

Dear Sir or Madam,

Information about the GRAND TOUR

Next August we __________ (visit) Scotland. We _________ (go) by car. My family and me, we are four persons, ____________ (arrive) in Edinburgh on Monday, 11 August.

We have heard about the famous castles and about your special offer – the GRAND TOUR. Hoping to find historic Scotland we __________ (do) the castle tour. What castles ____ we __________ (see)? We hope there __________ (be) a guide who ____________ (give) us some information about the castles. We are looking forward to listening to his stories. Perhaps he __________ (tell) us about the famous kings and queens and the howling ghosts – who knows!?

Could you send us further information about the GRAND TOUR, please. We are looking forward to hearing from you soon.

Yours faithfully ______________

A LETTER FROM CASTLE HOTEL

You inquired about accommodation at the 'Castle Hotel' in Braemar. A few weeks before your holidays you receive the following letter.

- Complete this letter from the hotel manager by filling in the missing positive or negative forms of the *will-future* or the *going to-future*.
- Compare your solutions with the answer key.

Castle Hotel Braemar

Dear guest,

Thank you for your inquiry about our Castle Hotel. We hope you ___________ (stay) in our house and would like to tell you about the activities in our hotel during your stay.

Our restaurant ___________ (stay) open an hour longer than in winter, but I can promise you that it ___________ (be) the only change.

There is a festival in Braemar during your stay and we ___________ (have) some special activities. We ___________ (have) a song evening with traditional Scottish music and we ___________ (organise) an evening with traditional games, which ___________ (be) open for non-residents.

We hope that you ___________ (enjoy) it.

Of course you can escape from the traditional activities that will take place in our hotel during the festival. You ___________ (not have to) sing songs that you don't know or like and you needn't worry that you ___________ (have to) play party games. It ___________ (be) an informal programme.

At the same time, we are sure you ___________ (experience) that our traditional and historic atmosphere is a very friendly one.

Please arrange your visit early. During the festival we ___________ (have) a lot of guests.

Yours sincerely,
Peter Black, Manager

QUESTIONS ABOUT CASTLES AND GHOSTS

You want to get some information about castles and ghosts.

- Work with a partner.
- Complete the questions using the *going to-future* or the *will-future*.
- Put the questions to your partner.
- Your partner has to give the right answer.
- Compare your solutions with the answer key.

Questions: **Answers:**

1. Which castles ___________ you _______________ (see) on the GRAND TOUR?	5. ________ you _______________ (watch) the exercises of the Atholl Highlanders at Blair Castle?	We are going to see …	Yes, we are going to watch …
2. ________ you _______________ (change) the GRAND TOUR and visit Muchalls Castle, too?	6. ________ you _______________ ______ (visit) Holyrood Palace during your stay in Edinburgh?	No, we aren't going to visit …	Yes, we are going to visit …
3. _________ you _______________ ___________ (stay) in a castle hotel in your next holidays?	7. _______ there _______________ (be) a lot of people with you on your guided GRAND TOUR?	Yes, we are going to stay …	I don't know, if there will be …
4. When ________ ____________ the Royals probably ____________ (be) in Balmoral next year?	8. ____________ you ____________ _______________ (ask) for the ghost story at Muchalls Castle?	They'll be there …	Yes, I'm going to ask …

A NIGHT IN AN OLD CASTLE (I)

Imagine – You are on the GRAND TOUR of Scotland. You are visiting a castle.
The owner of the castle tells you what is special about the ghosts that "live" there.

- Take a look at the pictures.
- Write a ghost story with the words given under the pictures.
- Write the story on a notepad first. Your teacher will then correct it.
- Glue the pictures into your exercise book.
- Write the story under the pictures in your exercise book.
- Compare your solution with the answer key.

Material: notepad, pictures

Mac Alister – at midnight – will appear

will go through – the locked door – he – of the secret chamber

A NIGHT IN AN OLD CASTLE (II)

along – he – the long hall – will move

his friend – he – at two minutes past twelve – will meet – Mac Arthur – where – they – at the castle tower – will howl

they – two minutes later – will play – on tourists – tricks

your alarm clock – will ring – they – splash water – or – in your face

will take – sometimes – they – your clothes away

will disappear – at a quarter past twelve – again – the two ghosts

SCOTTISH SPORTS

- Read the text.
  Look up any new words and write them into your exercise book.

A lot of visitors come to Scotland to play sports. They like to go fishing in the clear rivers and lakes, they go sailing or take boat trips on the lakes or along the coast. Some of them go walking in the Highlands or climbing in the mountains near Fort William. Skiing in Glenshee, hunting in the moors, riding in the Lowlands or playing tennis are other popular sports for tourists in Scotland.
But most of the sportsmen come to practise one sport that is very Scottish: golf. Variations of this game were played across Europe but it were the Scots who established the official game. We don't know much about the origins in Scotland but what is known is that James II described golf as a danger for national security in 1457, because instead of practising shooting with bow and arrow the Scots liked to play golf.
Mary Stuart, however, was a passionate player and established golf later. She played on the famous golf course of "Bruntsfield" in Edinburgh daily. The first golf balls were made of leather and filled with feathers – so they were called "feathery". In 1900 the Scots invented the first ball made of rubber – it was called "guttie". Many golf courses are very traditional, such as the championship course of St. Andrews. Actually, St. Andrews has got four golf courses and they are always booked up. To get a chance as a guest golfer there is a daily ballot that determines who is allowed to play on the course that day.
Scotland is also famous for another sport that is called "Shinty". It is one of the oldest team games in the world. 2000 years ago, Irish men brought this sport to Scotland. They called it *Camanachd*. Nowadays it is only played in Scotland – especially in the Highlands. It's connected to ice hockey but you have to play it on the lawn. There are 12 players in a team. They use a curved stick and have to hit a ball (the size of a tennis ball) into the goal of the opponent as often as possible. The players may hit the ball on the ground or over their heads – which sometimes looks a bit dangerous.

- Look at the sports signs below. Which kinds of sport are shown in the pictures? Use your dictionary if you don't know the sports.
- Compare your solution with the answer key.

Material: dictionary, sport signs

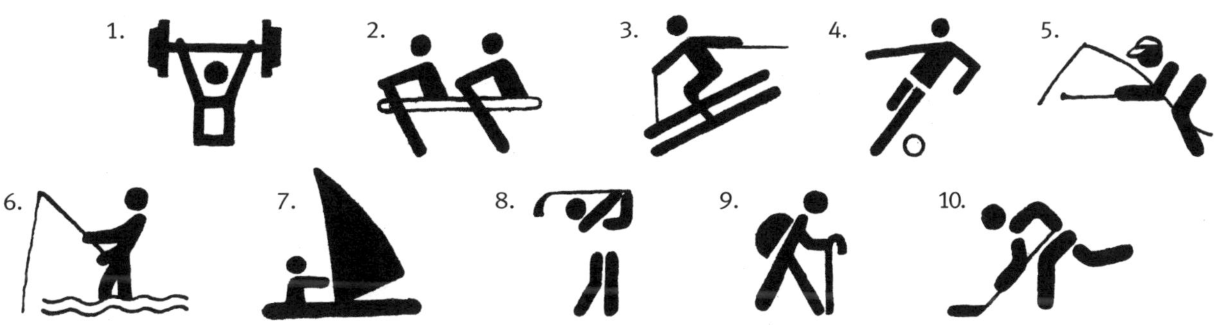

SIMPLE PRESENT

KEEP FIT – DAILY SPORTS

In order to keep fit sportsmen have to do sports daily. They have to do exercises.

Write down the missing forms of the *simple present* first.
Then find them in the puzzle. Compare your solution with the answer key.

1. It plays – they ____________
2. We watch – she ____________
3. You go – she ____________
4. We do – he ____________
5. She climbs – I ____________
6. They fish – he ____________
7. They fly – it ____________
8. He likes – you ____________
9. He tries – we ____________
10. You study – she ____________

A	Q	B	W	C	E	D	R	E	T	E	Z	F	U	G	I	H	O	J
P	K	P	L	M	G	A	N	S	O	D	L	I	K	E	P	F	Q	G
H	A	L	B	J	C	O	K	D	L	E	Y	F	X	G	C	H	V	I
J	B	A	N	K	M	L	E	W	M	E	N	R	O	T	P	Z	Q	U
I	R	Y	O	S	P	T	A	S	U	S	V	D	W	F	X	G	Y	H
Z	A	C	B	A	B	F	W	A	Y	E	W	P	A	P	A	S	D	F
A	S	F	H	U	C	E	E	S	X	W	A	T	C	H	E	S	W	Z
W	D	G	Z	P	L	G	R	D	C	T	A	I	B	W	E	R	T	Z
E	F	H	U	M	I	N	T	F	V	Z	S	U	C	U	I	O	P	A
R	G	U	U	V	M	N	Z	T	R	Y	D	Z	D	S	D	F	F	G
T	H	D	I	W	B	K	U	G	B	U	F	T	E	B	I	O	K	V
Z	J	Z	O	T	C	S	T	U	D	I	E	S	F	S	U	L	U	B
U	K	U	D	E	D	M	I	H	N	I	H	A	H	E	J	J	Z	N
I	L	P	W	Z	S	K	O	J	M	O	K	E	P	R	M	Z	T	M
O	W	K	N	X	G	O	P	K	Z	P	S	C	G	T	H	P	R	K
P	F	L	I	E	S	P	A	L	I	M	L	B	J	Z	G	W	E	O

What can you say about these Scottish sportsmen?
- Work with a partner: Tell your partner about Brenda and Tom.
- Then change roles: Your partner will tell you about Susan and Duncan.
- Compare your solution with the answer key.

<table>
<tr><td>+ sailing
– walking
volleyball
Braemar
Scotland</td><td>London
golf
+ fishing
– bowling
England</td><td>– hunting
Cardiff
+ skiing
Wales
tennis</td><td>Scotland
Shinty
+ soccer
– riding
Pitlochry</td></tr>
<tr><td colspan="4">comes from
lives
plays
+ likes
– hates</td></tr>
<tr><td>Brenda</td><td>Tom</td><td>Susan</td><td>Duncan</td></tr>
</table>

SIMPLE PRESENT **STATION B3**

SCOTTISH SPORTS ARE DIFFERENT!

Foreign people sometimes don't know enough about Scottish sports.

- Correct the statements. Write the correct sentences into your exercise book. Make the sentences negative, otherwise they won't make sense! Example: *She likes to go climbing in the mountains. No, she doesn't like to go climbing in the mountains, she likes to go pony-trekking.*
- Compare your solution with the answer key.

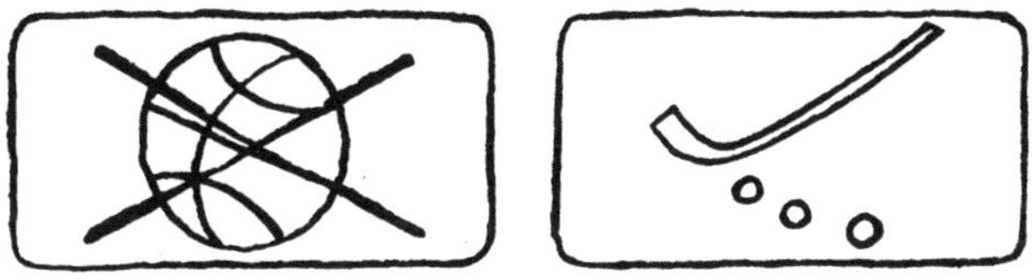

< 1. The Scottish like basketball! No, they … .

2. They like to go fishing in the Thames! No, they … . >

< 3. A traditional Scotsman likes to play table tennis! No, he … .

4. A Shinty player uses a broom! No, he … . >

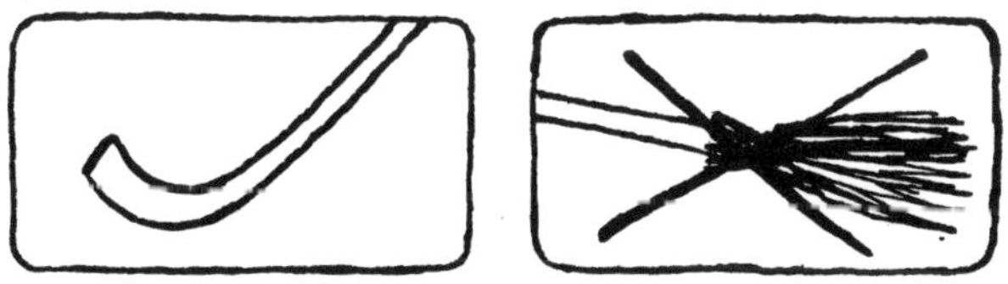

< 5. A lot of guests play handball in St. Andrews! No, they … .

6. The Scots like to practise bow and arrow like Robin Hood! No, they … . >

< 7. The daily ballot chooses a person who will win 100 pounds! No, it … .

8. The Shinty players play the ball on ice! No, they … . >

FINDING A SPORTING PARTNER (I)

Are you and your friend as sporting as Scottish sportsmen?

■ Fill in the table "That's me" and complete the questions about your opinion.
- Compare your solution with the answer key.
- "What is your opinion"? Mark your personal answers (yes or no) with a cross. Who has got the same number of points? Is it your ideal sporting partner?

That's me *(Here's room for a photo of you!)*	Name: ______________________ Birthday: ______________________ Address: ______________________ Sisters or brothers: ______________________ Hobbies: ______________________ Favourite Subjects at school: ______________________ ______________________

Sports: *(Here's room for a photo or a picture of your favourite sports!)*	What is your opinion about sports?	yes	no
	_______ you _______ (prefer) playing sports to watching TV?	1	0
	_______ you _______ (think) it's enough to do sports only once a month?	0	1
	_______ you _______ (feel) healthy if you do sports?	1	0
	_______ you _______ (know) two sports you'd like to do?	1	0
	_______ you _______ (prefer) playing sports all alone?	0	1
	_______ you _______ (think) men are better golf players than women?	0	1

FINDING A SPORTING PARTNER (II)

Are you and your friend as sporting as Scottish sportsmen?

Make questions and compare your solution with the answer key.
- Try to answer the questions for your best friend.
- Then put the questions to your friend. Mark the correct answers with a cross. Did you guess right – did you know if he/she is a sportsman/ sportswoman?

That's my friend
(Here's room for a photo of your friend!)

Name: ______

Birthday: ______

Address: ______

Sisters or brothers: ______

Hobbies: ______

Favourite Subjects at school: ______

______

Sports:
(Here's room for a photo or a picture of your friend's favourite sports!)

	My opinion		My friend's opinion	
I think that's his/ her opinion:	yes	no	yes	no
______ he/she ______ (prefer) playing sports to watching TV?	1	0		
______ he/she ______ (think) it's enough to do sports only once a month?	0	1		
______ he/she ______ (feel) healthy if he/she does sports?	1	0		
______ he/she ______ (know) two sports he'd/she'd like to do?	1	0		
______ he/she ______ (prefer) playing sports all alone?	0	1		
______ he/she ______ (think) men are better golf players than women?	0	1		

A SPORTING MAN

Mac Lachlan is a Scottish Lord. He is very proud.
Like other Scottish landlords he wants to be sporting.

- Try to write a story. The pictures and words below will help you.
- Compare your story with the answer key.

Material: Picture story

Mac Lachlan – Scottish landlord – proud – wants to be sporting – big aim: – win a sports cup – golf championships – St. Andrews – raining cats and dogs – not see the guttie – no points – no cup – but a cold

Mac Lachlan – Inverness Showjumping – tries to jump the first obstacle – horse stops – Mac Lachlan falls off – no cup – but broken arm

Mac Lachlan – Shinty – Shinty International Championships – raises the curved stick – does not get the ball – hits his head – hospital – bump on his head – but no cup

Mac Lachlan – Loch Lomond – fishing competition – row – boat – fishing-rod – something pulls him out of the boat – swallows a lot of water – gets a cold – but no cup

in winter – skiing – Highlands – downhill-racing – is fast – he has a fall – can't see Mac Lachlan – tips of his ski – broken leg – but no cup

at home – sitting in his armchair – open fire – proud – guess why – a cup – no sports cup – but: – cup for the most injured person of the year

THE HIGHLAND GAMES

- Read the text.
- Look up any new words in a dictionary.
  Write them down in your exercise-book.

Material: Dictionary, map

Every summer you can go to the Highland Games in different places in Scotland. They are also called “Oatmeal Olympics” and take place between May and September. Braemar is one of these places where you can watch the games every 1st Saturday in September.
The Braemar Royal Highland Gathering is famous because the Royal Family takes part in the games.
The games are hundreds of years old. In former times the games may have also served a military purpose by allowing the clan chiefs to choose the strongest men. Nowadays Scotland’s strongest men (who are also called the “heavies”) come together for different (fun) competitions. You can see a lot of strange sports that developed from country work, like “tossing the caber” (= lifting a tree trunk and throwing it into the air) “weight shifting” and “throwing the hammer”.
Tossing the caber is the most famous Highland sport. Originally the woodworkers had to take tree trunks to the nearest river and throw them into the river. Imagine: an average trunk is about 5,8 metres long and weighs about 54 kilograms! In the competition, the athlete must run with the tree trunk and toss (= throw) it in the way that it flips over 180° and lands vertically, straight ahead. Up to now they have only managed to do it three times. The referees judge the way the caber is thrown and not just the distance.
In order to show his strength in weight shifting the “heavy” must stand with his back to a bar, which he must throw the weight over. The bar is raised after each successful throw, until only one person is left in the competition.
Throwing the hammer: While circling the hammer (a weight at the end of a long pole) over his head, the sportsman gathers speed to throw the hammer far across the field.
There is also a lot of piping, singing and dancing going on at the Highland Games. Scotland’s best bagpipers come together and play their instruments. Bagpipes have been the traditional instrument of the Highlands for many centuries and were probably introduced by the Romans. The classical music is called Pibroch. Its slow and melancholy tunes are usually played by a solo piper.
Highland dancing is also an important part of the Highland Games and the dances often have a symbolic meaning. The circle, for example, symbolizes the circle of life.
In the morning the Scottish families come to the field where the Highland Games are held. They bring along blankets and picnic baskets and watch the games and dancing. It’s like a meeting of the different “clans”, the different Scottish families.

THE HIGHLAND GAMES – FIELD MAP

- Have a look at the map of the sports fields and read the list of activities at the bottom of the page.
- Write down the numbers and the matching activities in your exercise-book.

dancing – visitors – jury – solo pipers – barbecue – flea market – sheepdog show – facilities/ lavatory – sheep show – meals/drinks (refreshment stand) – athletic games – bagpiping bands

PRESENT PROGRESSIVE

WHAT ARE THEY DOING AT THE HIGHLAND GAMES?

There are a lot of activities at the Highland Games. Describe your picture to your partner:

- Your partner gets picture A, you get picture B.
- Don't look at your partner's picture.
- Tell your partner what the Scottish athletes are doing:
  Example: *An athlete is tossing the caber in picture A.*
- Your partner has to say if the sentence is correct for picture B:
  Example: *Yes, an athlete is tossing the caber, too (in picture B)* or
  No, three athletes are tossing the caber in picture B or
  No, nobody is tossing the caber in picture B.

Material: picture A and B

Picture A

Picture B

WHAT ARE THE "HEAVIES" DOING? (I)

The strongest men of Scotland practise strange sports.

- Work with a partner.
- Take 6 picture cards each.
- Look at the pictures – The keywords underneath the pictures aren't correct.
- Take it in turns to tell each other the correct solution:
  Example:
  You: "Mac Fraser isn't throwing the golf ball, he is throwing the caber."
  Your partner: "Peter isn't shifting the weight, he is ..."
- Compare your solution with the answer key.
- Variation: Take 1 picture card. Ask your partner what the people in the picture are doing. Your partner must answer. Then change roles.
  Example:
  You: "What is Susan doing?" – Your partner: "Susan is dancing."
  Your partner: "What are the farmers doing." – You: "..."

Material: pictures

Peter – shifting the weight

Arthur – pulling the rope

the farmers – dancing

the visitors – showing their best sheepdogs

PRESENT PROGRESSIVE

WHAT ARE THE "HEAVIES" DOING? (II)

5

Ben – throwing the hammer

6

the shepherds – looking at the sheep

7

Willi – tossing the caber

8

Susan and Ailean – playing the bagpipes

9

the Queen – eating a hot dog

10

Tom – fighting

11

Bill and Sam – putting the shot

12

the little girl – watching the games from the VIP-stand

HELP THE GERMANS TO UNDERSTAND THE EXPLANATIONS

Every year a lot of Germans visit the famous Highland Games but they often can't understand the explanations of the announcer.

- Listen to the cassette.
- Translate text A to your partner – your partner will translate text B to you.
- Variation: Can you formulate questions on the text? Use the present progressive. Put the questions to your partner:
  Example: *"What are they offering at the refreshment stand?"* –
  "They are offering tea and shortbread."
  "What is Mr MacDougall doing?" ...
- Compare your solution with the answer key.

Material: cassette recorder, cassette

Text A:

Dear guests,
I would like to welcome you to the 2002 Braemar Royal Highland Gathering.
We are starting with the games soon. In the North of the field you can watch the dancing of the young ladies. Mr MacDougall is playing his bagpipes for them.
Now you can see a 15 year old dancer, dancing the circle. In the west of the field there is a refreshment stand. There you can have warm tea, cold Scottish drinks and home-made shortbread. You can also order warm meals. In the east of the field you can visit the flea market. The stallholders (= Standinhaber) will be happy if you take a look at their goods.

Text B:

In the middle of the field we are starting the heavies' competition. We are starting with weight shifting. After that we will present circling the hammer and tossing the caber.
25 of our strongest Scottish men will be showing their strength.
The names of the sportsmen can be found in the programme as well as the rules of the different sports. There are four referees. They will make sure that the sportsmen keep to the rules. We hope you will enjoy your stay in Braemar. 'May the best man win!'

A TV-REPORT ABOUT THE BRAEMAR HIGHLAND GAMES

A reporter has taken some notes and wants to report live on TV. Can you help him?

- Write the TV-report into your exercise-book.
  Use the correct tenses – Remember: They are just playing.
- Compare your solutions with the answer key.
- Record your report on cassette.

Material: Cassette recorder, cassette

- Good afternoon Ladies and Gentlemen!
- Saturday, 4th September
- live-report
- Braemar Royal Highland Gathering
- referee Scott – waiting for the heavies

(Some minutes later)

- Aidan: tossing the caber – Conor: throwing the hammer

(Some minutes later)

- funny games: farmers – pulling the rope, teenagers – sack-racing
- dancers from 6 to 18 years – dancing traditional dances
- bagpiper Brian O'Neill – playing his bagpipes
- the local women at the refreshment stand – offering delicious meals: barbecued meat, hot dogs, salads, corn on the cob, sandwiches, home-made cakes, tea
- Queen, Royal Family – spending their summer holidays
- joining the crowd at the Highland Games – show(ing) interest in Scottish activities

KILTS AND CLANS

- Read the text.
- Look up any new words in your dictionary.
  Write them down in your exercise book.
- Find Culloden on the map.

Have you ever seen a man in a skirt? – In Scotland it's traditional and those skirts are called kilts. Crossing a river in the old days was easier in a kilt than in trousers. The trousers would have been wet for some hours – not so the kilt. Until the battle of Culloden the kilt was the everyday outfit of all men. Why is Culloden connected with the tradition of wearing a kilt? In 1745 Bonnie Prince Charlie (Charles Edward Stuart) wanted to claim the British Crown. So he led the Scottish rebellions against the British government army.
In 1746, there was a battle on Culloden Moor but the Scots were defeated. Bonnie Prince Charlie fled to France and as a result of the defeat the Scots were forbidden to wear a kilt, to have bagpipes or to carry weapons. For several years, they had to live without their traditional music and – what was even worse – they had to wear trousers.
In those days the Scots lived together as "Clans". In Gaelic, the word "clan" means "family" or "children". Those clans were groups who were led by a chief, the tribal father, and bore his name although they weren't related by blood. Today you can still identify the clans by looking at their famous names: The MacDonalds, the Frazers, the Stuarts and the MacKenzies. And even today, every clan has its own kilt with special colours and a special pattern or set. Those kilts are made of a special cloth called "tartan". There are "big kilts" (fealeadh mor) and "small kilts" (feileadh beg). It's surprising that you need about 5 metres of cloth for the traditional big kilt.
The big kilt is a skirt with one ending thrown over the shoulder. The small kilt doesn't have the cloth over the shoulder and is preferred nowadays. Today it is only worn on official celebrations and at the Highland Games. Although the clans only exist by name today, they are very proud of their past. They show their pride in wearing the kilt and the accessories as shown in the picture.

- Cut out the pictures, glue them into your exercise book and write the correct English word under each picture. Here are some clues: a tie, a tweed-jacket, woollen stockings, a belt with the sporran (= a special bag belonging to the kilt), a scarf (worn over the shoulder), a dagger/dirk (hidden in the left stocking).

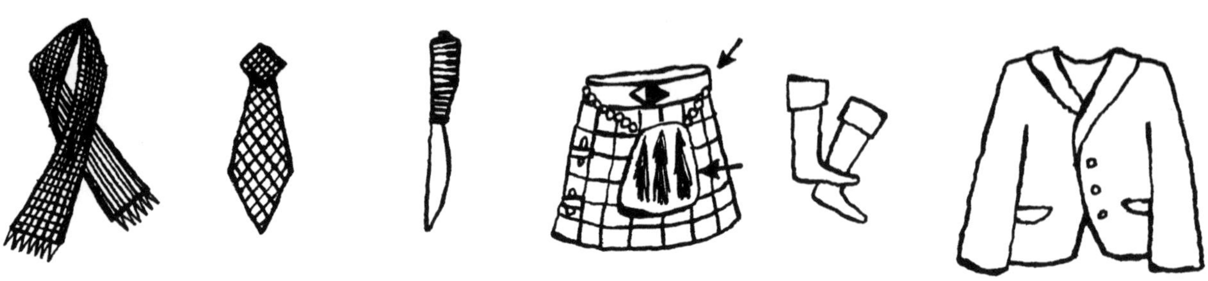

PRESENT PERFECT

MEETING THE FRAZER CLAN

Once a year there is a meeting of the Frazer Clan in Culloden.
A reporter is there, too.

■ Read the sentences and mark the right form of "to have" with a cross.

	has	have
1. I __________ met Peter Frazer, the chief of the clan.	______	______
2. We __________ met at Clan meetings before.	______	______
3. We __________ already visited the Culloden Battle Field.	______	______
4. The Frazers __________ never been to the USA.	______	______
5. They __________ always stayed in Scotland.	______	______
6. Peter's wife __________ organized the meeting.	______	______
7. She __________ prepared the picnic lunch.	______	______
8. I __________ never taken part in meetings of other clans.	______	______

■ When do you use FOR and SINCE?

Easter   my last birthday

two weeks   centuries   1745   five days

our last meeting   eight months   Christmas

the battle of Culloden   thirty minutes   their wedding day

■ Make a list. Fill in the terms.

since	for
January	...

■ Compare your solution with the answer key

TRUE OR FALSE? FACTS ABOUT SCOTLAND

The kilt is something special in Scotland – now you have some knowledge about it.

- Have a look at the speech bubbles. Do you agree with the statements? If not, make the sentences negative.
- Compare your solution with the answer key.

Interview: Find out what your partner knows about Scotland.

- Ask questions in the *present perfect.*
  Be careful: You must fill in the *past participle* of the verbs *(in brackets)*.
- Put the questions to your partner:
  Example:
  You: "Have you ever worn a kilt?" –
  Your partner: "No, I haven't." – or: "Yes, I have."

Have you ever ...?

– *(wear)* a kilt
– *(be)* to Scotland
– (visit) a tartan store
– (see) the various clan patterns
– ...

– *(hear)* about the 'Battle of Culloden'
– (read) a book about the Highlanders
– (watch) a film about Bonnie Prince Charlie

AT A WOOLLEN MILL

You and your friend are at a woollen mill. You are listening to a conversation but your friend doesn't understand what the customer and the shop assistant are saying to each other.

- Translate the dialogue to your friend.
- Write the translation into your exercise book.
- Compare it with the answer key.

Hello, can I help you? →	← I'd like to try on a kilt.
Have you ever worn a kilt? →	No, I have never worn a kilt before. ← Up to now, I have always worn trousers.
The Scots have always worn the kilt together with a tweed jacket, a belt, a sporran and a dagger. →	I have just seen a man dressed like that at the Highland Games. ... Have you got any ← information about the patterns?
Well, yes, I have. Even today, every clan has got its own individual kilt with special colours and a special pattern or set. Those kilts are made of a cloth called "tartan". You can find some of the most popular Clan patterns in our brochure. →	Thank you, that's very interesting. Now I'd really like to buy ← a kilt as a souvenir.
What about the kilt over there – the one with the dark green and yellow pattern? That would suit you well. →	... Yes, I think I'll take it. ← How much is it?

HOW TO WEAR A "BIG" KILT

The traditional way of putting on a big kilt:

1. Put the belt on the floor.
2. Place the cloth on the belt.
3. The lower part must have the length from waist to knee.
4. Lie down on the cloth.
5. Fold the cloth so that the edges overlap and close the belt.
6. Throw the upper part of the cloth over your left shoulder (from behind).
7. Fix the cloth on the left shoulder with a brooch.
8. Tuck the end of the cloth through the belt.

In the pictures above you can see John McNally preparing for his visit to the Highland games. Look at the pictures and describe what McNally has just done.

- Read the instructions on "how to wear a big kilt" (see above!).
- Look at the jumbled sentences below.
- Write down the sentences in the correct order. Use the *present perfect*.
- Compare your solution with the answer key.

Introduction: have always worn – members of a clan – the big kilt –
that's why – has decided – McNally – to put on a big kilt – for his visit – to the Highland Games

a. has put – McNally – a belt – on the floor
b. has placed – the cloth – on the belt – he
c. has measured – according to the length from waist to knee – the lower part of the cloth – he
d. has lain down – on the cloth – McNally
e. he – so that the edges overlap – and he has closed the belt – has folded the cloth
f. over the left shoulder – has thrown – the upper part of the cloth – McNally
g. with a brooch – he – has fixed – on the left shoulder – the cloth
h. has tucked – the end of the cloth – he – through the belt

... Now McNally is fully dressed and ready to go to the Highland Games!

SCOTTISH INVENTIONS

- Read the text.
- Look up the unknown words in the dictionary.
  Write down the new words in your exercise book.

Despite its small size and low population Scotland has produced some important inventors over the centuries. In the 18th and 19th century many technological, medical and mechanical discoveries were made there, including the invention of logarithm tables (by John Napier in 1594), the preservation of marmalade (by Janet Keiller in 1797) and the discovery of continuous electric light (by James Bowman Lindsay in 1834) as well as the development of the thermos flask (by James Dewar in 1892), the pneumatic tyre (by John Dunlop in 1888) and the refrigerator (by James Harrison in 1856).
Apart from these there are some other really outstanding inventions that caused a breakthrough: In 1782 James Watt invented the rotative steam engine. It was the refinement of the existing steam engine that caused the Industrial Revolution.
In 1839, Kirkpatrick Macmillan developed the first pedal-powered bicycle. It was based on the foot-powered "velocipede" and allowed people to cover longer distances in a shorter time. In the following years, Macmillan's great invention was copied and manufactured in large numbers.
The Scottish physicist James C. Maxwell developed colour photography in 1861. The subject shown in his first three-colour photograph was his tartan ribbon.
Alexander Graham Bell, a man from Edinburgh, invented the telephone in 1876. It was a scientific breakthrough for communication all around the world.
Penicillin is a discovery that has changed the face of medicine. In 1928 Alexander Fleming's first idea was to treat diseases. But in 1940, Penicillin helped to save the lives of thousands of wounded soldiers.
In 1926 John Logie Baird invented a black and white TV. It couldn't produce sound and pictures at the same time but nevertheless it was a great invention.
A team of scientists at Edinburgh's Roslin Institute succeeded in cloning the sheep "Dolly" in 1996. Dolly was the clone of an adult sheep and gave birth to lamb "Bonnie" in 1998. Dolly died in 2003.

- Draw a time line and fill in the dates and events.

Material: dictionary

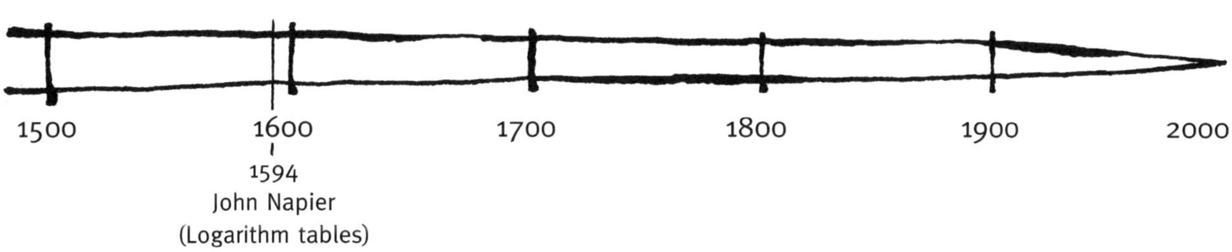

WHAT DID THE INVENTORS DO?

■ Fill in the *simple past* and the *past participle* of the verbs.
Compare your solution with the answer key.

(to) produce		have/has
(to) cause		have/has
(to) invent		have/has
(to) manufacture		have/has
(to) allow		have/has
(to) develop		have/has
(to) change		have/has

(to) make		have/has
(to) be		have/has
(to) give		have/has

- Play “verb rummy” with two partners:
- Write each verb form onto a file card (= Karteikarte).
- Each of you gets 6 cards; all the other cards are in the middle of the table upside down on a pile.
- Begin by taking one card from the pile.
- You may keep the card or put it back. If you keep it, you must put back a different card from your hand. Now it’s your partner’s turn.
- The aim of the game is to arrange all the cards in your hand into sets of 3. Each set must contain the *infinitive*, *simple past* and *past participle* forms of the same verb.
- A round ends when one player has spread two matching sets of 3 cards on the table. The winner gets a point.

■ What did the inventors do? Talk to your friends about Scottish inventions.
- Take the *simple past*-cards of the verbs and share them out among you and your partners.
- Make a sentence with each card, giving information about an invention (if you don’t know any more the text E1: “Scottish Inventions” will help you).
  Example: “invented” – *The Scottish invented a lot of things.*

ARE THESE THE RIGHT INVENTIONS?

Let's test your knowledge!

- Look at the tables below.
- Write down what the inventors did and didn't do.
  e.g. *John Napier didn't write a time table. He wrote the logarithm tables.*
- Compare your solution with the answer key.

John Napier		Janet Keiller		James Bowman Lindsay		James Dewar		John Dunlop	
write		preserve		produce		develop		discover	
a time-table	the logarithm tables	juice	marmalade	candle light	continuous electric light	glass bottle	thermos flask	wooden wheel	pneumatic tyres

James Harrison		James Watt		Kirkpatrick Macmillan		James C. Maxwell		Alexander GrahamBell	
invent		build		construct		take		communicate	
a heater	a refrigerator	a motor engine	a steam engine	a motor-bike	a pedal-powered bicycle	a black and white photo-graph	the first colour photo-graph	via the internet	by telephone

Alexander Fleming		John Logie Baird		Scientists at Roslin Institute	
discover		produce		clone	
a cough mixture	penicillin	a radio	a tele-vision	a goat	the sheep Dolly

TALKING ABOUT AN INVENTOR

The invention of the telephone

Although the telephone was invented in the USA, it was invented by a Scotsman: Mister Alexander Graham Bell.

- Read the text about Alexander Graham Bell.
- Look up any new words in your dictionary.
- Tell your friend about the invention of the telephone in German.

Alexander Graham Bell was born in Edinburgh, Scotland, on March 3, 1847.
He had always been interested in the study of sound and so he started to teach at university when he was 16. At the age of twenty-six he moved to Boston, USA, and worked as a professor at Boston University. His aim was to transmit words electronically. He constructed a new type of transmitter and made a lot of experiments.
In March 1876 he sent his assistant Watson to a different room on the next floor of the building – far away from him. While Bell was assembling the last parts of his telephone, some battery acid dripped onto his trousers. He called for his assistant Watson. Through the instrument, Watson heard the following words:

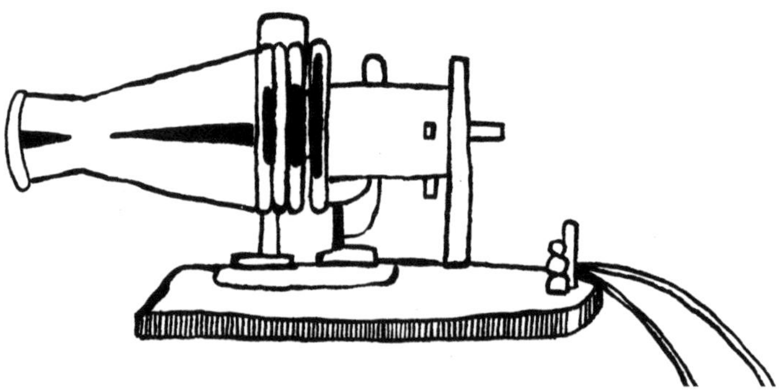

"Mr Watson, come here. I want you!", and Watson went to Bell's room. It was a great invention.
In 1892 Watson and Bell made their first telephone call from New York to Chicago and 23 years later they made their first call from the east to the west coast.

Talking about an inventor: a puzzle

You meet a Scotsman. You are interested in Bell's life and his invention, so you ask a lot of questions.

- Each answer-card corresponds to a question on the board. Put the right answer-card onto the board.
- The shapes given on the board will help you in case you don't know if you are right.

Material: answer-cards, board

TALKING ABOUT AN INVENTOR (ANSWER CARDS)

- He was born on March 3, 1847.
- He started teaching at the age of 16.
- It was Watson.
- He moved to the USA in 1873.
- He was born in Edinburgh, Scotland.
- They made their first telephone call from New York to Chicago in 1892.
- He was interested in the study of sound.
- Alexander Graham Bell said the first words.
- He already taught at university at the age of 16.
- He worked as a professor.
- Watson was on the next floor of the building.
- He moved to Boston in 1873.
- He wanted to transmit words electronically.
- He invented the telephone in March 1876.
- He worked at Boston University.
- They made their first call from the east to the west coast in 1915.
- He said: "Mr Watson, come here. I want you!"
- He was assembling the last parts of this telephone and some battery acid dripped onto his trousers.

TALKING ABOUT AN INVENTOR (PUZZLE BOARD)

When was Alexander Graham Bell born?

When did Bell start teaching at university?

Who was Bell's assistant?.

When did Bell move to the USA?

Where was A. G. Bell born?

When did Bell and Watson make their first telephone call from New York to Chicago?

What was Bell interested in?

Who said the first words via the telephone?

What did Bell do at the age of 16?

What did Bell work as in Boston?

Where was Watson when he heard Bell for the first time?

Where did A. G. Bell move to in 1873?

When did A. G. Bell invent the telephone?

Where did A. G. Bell work in Boston?

What was Bell's aim in Boston?

When did Watson and Bell make the first call from the east to the west coast?

What did Bell say on the telephone the first time?

What was Bell doing when Watson heard him for the first time?

A STORY ABOUT THE INVENTION OF THE PEDAL-BIKE

The velocipede was the first bike. It was invented by a German.

- Write the story about the invention of the bike:
- Put the words of the jumbled sentences into the right order.
- Write the story into your exercise book.
- Compare your solution with the answer key.

The invention of the pedal-bike

1. the German baron – built – a two-wheel bike – Karl Friedrich Christian Ludwig Drais von Sauerbronn
2. had to sit – and walk – he – on the saddle
3. was called – his invention – “velocipede”
4. helped – people – four times faster – on foot only – the velocipede – to move – than
5. was used – the velocipede – until 1839
6. added – Kirkpatrick Macmillan – that moved – two pedals – the back wheel – in 1939
7. allowed – to cover – this pedal–powered bicycle – in a shorter time – people – longer distances
8. became – popular – it – very
9. was manufactured – it – in large numbers – that is why

LOCH NESS AND NESSIE

- Read the text and look up the unknown words.
- Write down the new words in your exercise book.
- What do you think – is there a "Nessie"?
  Discuss your opinion with your partner.

If you go to Inverness you can't miss the famous Loch Ness. Loch Ness is a lake in Scotland – the biggest of all Scottish lakes. It's 24 miles long, 1 mile wide and a thousand feet deep – deeper than the North Sea. Loch Ness is famous all over the world for the monster "Nessie" that is supposed to live there.

It cannot be said with certainty whether there is a monster in Loch Ness or not – some people say YES, others say NO.
Those who believe in the monster think that it is millions of years old.
In 1934 doctor Robert Wilson from London was driving round Loch Ness while on holiday when he saw something very unusual break the surface. He reached for his camera and took four photos. The famous photos show something with a long neck and a small head.

In the sixties Mr Campbell and Mr MacIntyre were sitting in a small boat on Loch Ness. Suddenly they noticed something big swimming in the lake. They said that its head had been bigger than a cow's head and that it had frightened them.

In the 1980s the American University started a project to find the monster. They sent a team with modern technology, submarines and underwater cameras. But as Loch Ness is very long and the water is very dark because of the peat, the divers couldn't see very far. But they took three photos showing a shadow of about six to nine metres in length.

People who believe that there is no monster in Loch Ness say that Nessie is only a wave or the sun's reflection. They think that hotel managers invented Nessie for the tourists in order to fill their hotels.
Is Nessie a mammal *(= Säugetier)* or a beast of prey *(= Raubtier)*? Mammals would have to come to the surface regularly in order to breathe and beasts of prey couldn't find food in Loch Ness. So it remains a mystery if there is a monster in Loch Ness or not.
What do you think?

THE LOCH NESS MONSTER EXHIBITION (I)

In Drumnadrochit there is a special exhibition about the Loch Ness Monster.

Trimino:

- Try to find the *past participle*:
- Match the *infinitive* of the verb given on one side of a triangle with the corresponding *past participle* of the verb on another triangle.
- If you put all the triangles together correctly they will form a bigger triangle.

Material: Trimino

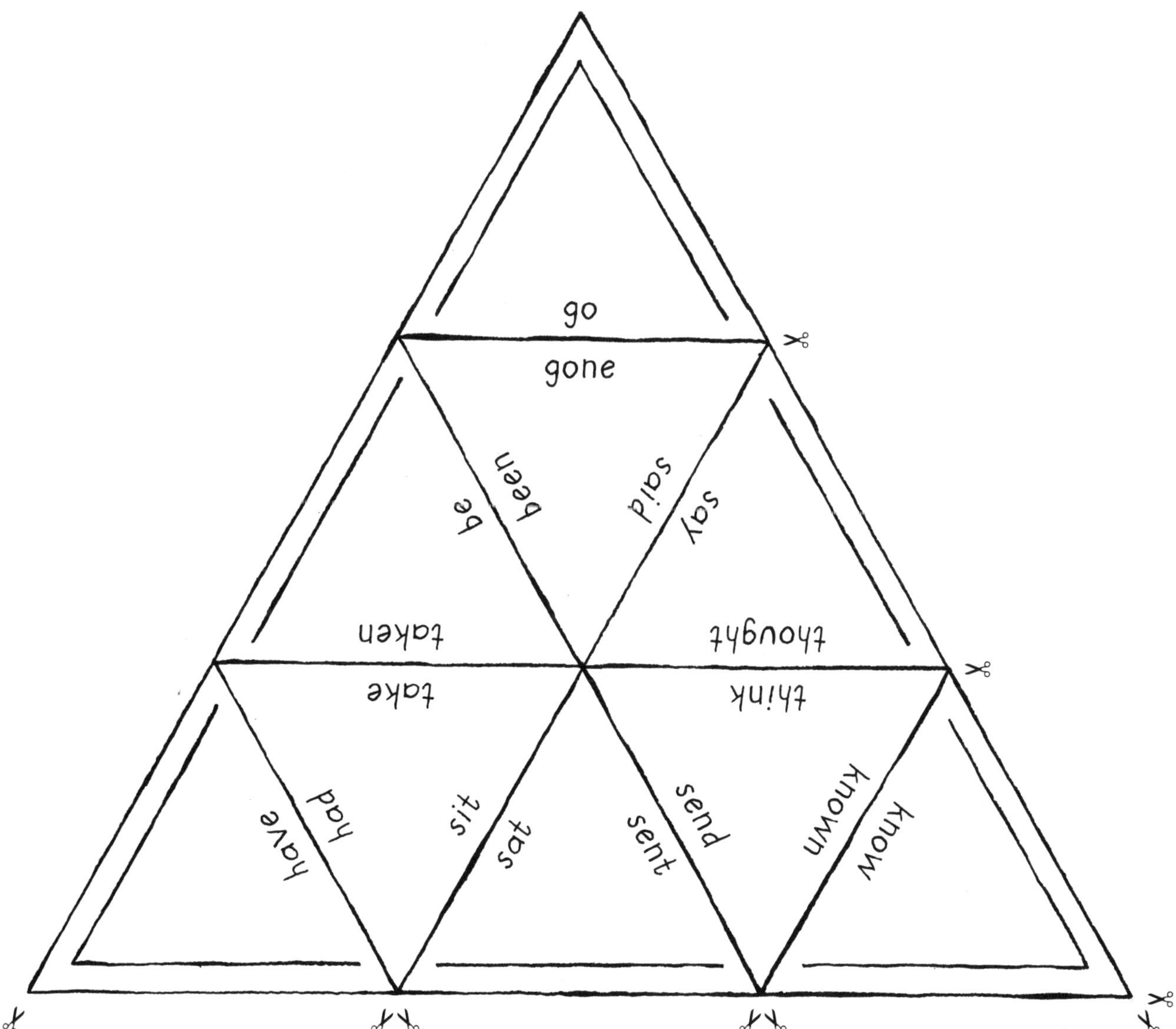

THE LOCH NESS MONSTER EXHIBITION (II)

Peter is interested in the Nessie Exhibition. He starts from Inverness to get to Drumnadrochit.

■ Read the report about Peter's trip:

a. As soon as Peter had organised the trip to Drumnadrochit, he looked for the right bus.
b. As soon as he had arrived at Loch Ness, he visited the museum shop.
c. After he had noticed that he was in the wrong room, he went to the entrance of the museum.
d. After he had bought an entrance ticket he went to the meeting point.
e. But he got to the meeting point for the guided tour late and when he arrived, the tour guide had already left.
f. After Peter had spoken to the attendant he started the tour on his own.
g. As soon as he had seen the geological exhibition about Loch Ness he met the guided tour.
h. Peter was very interested in explanations after he had heard that there were photographs showing a monster.

■ In each of the sentences above there are two actions that happened at different times.
■ What happened first? Which action came second?
■ Make a list:
Example: Peter left Inverness right after he had had breakfast.

First	Second
Example: had had breakfast	*left*
a. had organised	...
b.	
c.	
c.	
d.	
e.	
f.	
g.	
h.	

■ Compare your solution with the answer key.

THE NESSIE GAME (RULES)

- Play with your classmates.
- Throw the dice and move the correct number of spaces.
- Whenever you land on a "?"-space someone takes a question card and asks you a question. If your answer is correct you may throw the dice again. If your answer is wrong you have to move back three spaces.
- If your counter lands on one of your opponent's they are knocked off and returned to the START.
- If you land on a Nessie-joker you are allowed to move two spaces forward.
- The winner is the first player to reach the FINISH space.

Material: game, dice, counter (= Spielstein), question cards.

Cut out the questions cards below:

1 What did the two men notice when they had rowed their boat to the middle of the lake?	**2** What had doctor Wilson seen before he reached for his camera?
3 Why had the doctor taken his camera before he started to drive round Loch Ness?	**4** What did the American University do when they had heard about the strange animal?
5 What did the American students find after they had brought submarines with underwater cameras into Loch Ness?	**6** How did Mr Campbell and Mr McIntyre feel after they had seen the strange head?
7 What did the divers of the American University see on the photos after they had developed their films?	**8** What did the hotel managers do after they had heard about the strange animal?
9 What was the creature called after it had been proclaimed a monster?	**10** Why didn't the scientists see anything although their equipment had been professional underwater equipment?
11 Why did the biologists think it wasn't possible that there was a monster after they had made their experiments?	**12** Why did they make an exhibition about Nessie even though they hadn't found a monster?
13 Why had Loch Ness always been famous?	**14** What did people believe after the scientists hadn't found a monster?
15 What did the scientists find after they had started the "Operation Deepscan" in 1987?	**16** Why did people believe Dr. Wilson that he had seen a monster?

THE NESSIE GAME

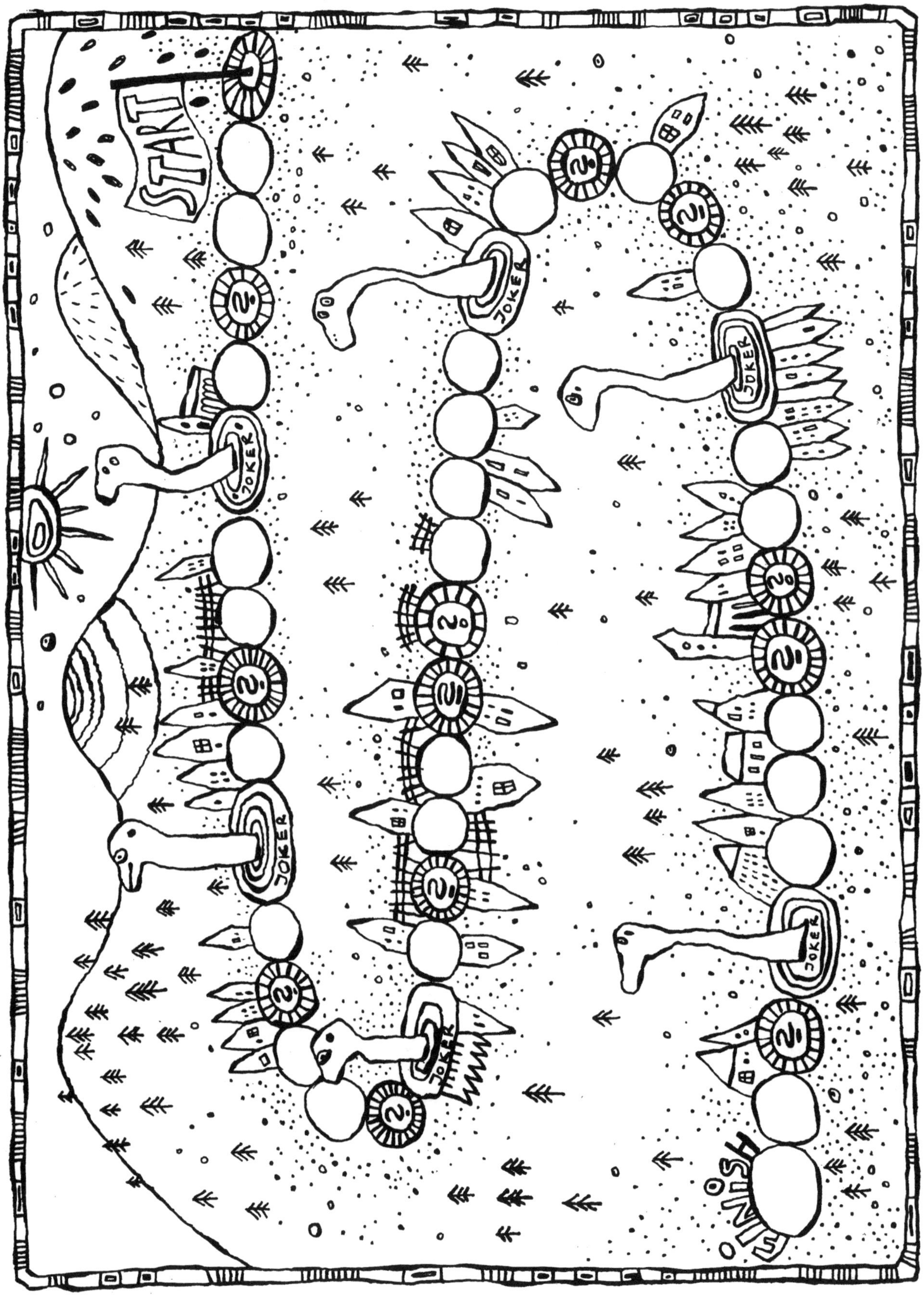

NESSIE IS JOKING

- Translate the jokes about Nessie into German.
- Compare your solution with the answer key.

a. At home at Nessie's house

Mother:	Nessie-Baby, did you give the fish in the tank fresh water after you had fed them?
Nessie-Baby:	No, Mummy, they hadn't drunk the water from the last time yet.

b. Nessie's hobby: driving a motor boat

Policeman:	We followed you right after you had started your motor boat. You were driving 200 km per hour.
Nessie:	Oh, isn't that great. – I only learnt how to drive a motor boat yesterday.

c. Meeting friends

Nessie:	I saw a tourist yesterday who I hadn't seen for twenty years.
Sharky:	That's nothing. I have just met somebody who I haven't seen in my whole life.

d. Absent-minded Nessie

Ducky:	Nessie, did you enjoy your bath after you had frightened the tourists?
Nessie:	No, I had forgotten to take off my clothes before I got into the bath.
Ducky:	Oh dear, did you get wet?
Nessie:	No, I had forgotten to put water into the tub!

A POSTCARD FROM LOCH NESS

After you had seen Inverness you visited Loch Ness. Write a postcard to your friend. Tell your friend what happened after you had done something else.

- You might use the following words: after ..., as soon as ... ..., before ..., ..., when ...
- Compare your solution with the answer key.

ANSWER KEY

A 2

are going to visit, are going to go, will arrive/ are going to arrive, will do/are going to do, will ... see/are ... going to see, will be, will give/ is going to give, will tell

A 3

are going to stay/will stay, will stay/is going to stay, will be, are going to have/will have, are going to have/will have, are going to organise/ will organise, will be/is going to be, will enjoy, won't have to, will have to, will be, will experience, will have

A 4

are ... going to see, Are ... going to change, Are ... going to stay, will ... be, Are ... going to watch, Are ... going to visit, Will ... be, Are ... going to ask

A 5

At midnight Mac Alister will appear.
He will go through the locked door of the secret chamber.
He will move along the long hall. At two minutes past twelve he will meet his friend Mac Arthur at the castle tower where they will howl.
Two minutes later they will play tricks on tourists.
Your alarm clock will ring or they will splash water in your face.
Sometimes they will take your clothes away.
At a quarter past twelve the two ghosts will disappear again.

B 1

1. weightlifting, 2. rowing, 3. skiing, 4. playing football, 5. riding, 6. fishing, 7. sailing, 8. playing golf, 9. walking/hiking, 10. playing Shinty

B 2

play, watches, goes, does, climb, fishes, flies, like, try, studies
Brenda comes from Scotland. She lives in Braemar. She plays volleyball. Brenda likes sailing, but she hates walking.
Tom comes from England. He lives in London. He plays golf. Tom likes fishing but he hates bowling.
Susan comes from Wales. She lives in Cardiff. She plays tennis. Susan likes skiing but she hates hunting.
Duncan is from Scotland. He lives in Pitlochry. He plays Shinty. Duncan likes soccer but he hates riding.

B 3

No, they don't like basketball, they like golf.
No, they don't like fishing in the Thames, they like fishing in the lakes.
No, he doesn't like to play table tennis, he likes to play Shinty.
No, a Shinty player doesn't use a broom, he uses a curved stick.
No, the guests don't play handball in St. Andrews, they play golf.
No, they don't like to practise (with) bow and arrow like Robin Hood, they like to practise golf.
No, the daily ballot doesn't choose a person who will win 100 pounds, it chooses the players for that day.
No, the Shinty players don't play the ball on ice, they play it on the ground or in the air.

B 4

Do ... prefer ..., Do ... think ..., Do ... know ..., Do ... prefer ..., Do ... think ...

Does ... prefer ..., Does ... think ..., Does ... feel ..., Does ... know ..., Does ... prefer ..., Does ... think ...

B 5

Mac Lachlan is a Scottish landlord. He is very proud and he wants to be sporting. His big aim is to win a sports cup. He takes part in the golf championships at St. Andrews. But soon it starts raining cats and dogs. Mac Lachlan can't see the guttie anymore and doesn't score any points. He hasn't got the cup but he has got a cold.
Mac Lachlan takes part in the Inverness Showjumping. He tries to jump the first obstacle, but his horse stops. Mac Lachlan falls off (flies through the air and lands on the ground). He hasn't got a cup but he has got a broken arm.
Mac Lachlan tries the old game of Shinty at the Shinty International Championships. He raises the curved stick to strike the ball. But unfortunately he doesn't get the ball (But instead of getting the ball) – he hits his head. He has to go to hospital because he has got a bump on his head ... but (he still has) no cup!
Mac Lachlan enters the (goes to the) Loch Lomond fishing competition. He rows his boat into the middle of the Loch and casts/throws his fishing-rod. Suddenly something pulls him out of the boat. He swallows a lot of water. He gets a bad cold but no cup.
In winter the landlord goes skiing in the Highlands. He takes part in a downhill-racing. He is fast but suddenly he has a fall. You can't see Mac Lachlan

ANSWER KEY

anymore, but you can see the tips of his ski.
He has got a broken leg but no sports cup.
At home again he is sitting in his armchair by the open fire and he is very proud. Guess why! He has got/(won) a cup! It's not a sports cup – (but) it's the cup for the most injured person of the year.

C 1

1. solo pipers
2. dancing
3. visitors
4. athletic games
5. barbecue
6. bagpiping bands
7. sheepdog show
8. meals/drinks (refreshment stand)
9. sheep show
10. flea market
11. jury/referees
12. facilities/lavatory

C 3

1. Peter isn't shifting the weight, he is tossing the caber.
2. Arthur isn't pulling the rope, he is throwing the hammer.
3. The farmers aren't dancing, they are pulling the rope.
4. The visitors aren't showing their best sheepdogs, they are looking at the sheep.
5. Ben isn't throwing the hammer, he is playing the bagpipes.
6. The shepherds aren't looking at the sheep, they are showing their best sheepdogs.
7. Willi isn't tossing the caber, he is shifting the weight/weightshifting.
8. Susan and Ailean aren't playing the bagpipes, they are dancing.
9. The Queen isn't eating a hot dog, she is watching the games from the VIP-stand.
10. Tom isn't fighting, he is putting the shot.
11. Bill and Sam aren't putting the shot, they are fighting.
12. The little girl isn't watching the games from the VIP-stand, she is eating a hot dog.

C 4

Text A:
Liebe Gäste,
Ich möchte Sie herzlich zu den königlichen Hochlandspielen 2002 in Braemar begrüßen. Wir beginnen bald mit den Spielen. Im Norden des Geländes können Sie die Tänze der jungen Ladys beobachten. Herr MacDougall spielt seinen Dudelsack für sie. Gerade sehen Sie eine 15-jährige Tänzerin, die den Circle tanzt.
Im Westen des Geländes ist ein/(finden Sie einen) Erfrischungsstand. Hier können Sie warmen Tee, kalte schottische Getränke und hausgemachtes Shortbread haben/kosten. Außerdem können Sie auch warmes Essen bestellen.
Im Osten des Geländes finden Sie den Flohmarkt. Die Standinhaber/Teilnehmer freuen sich, wenn Sie ihre Waren ansehen.

Text B:
In der Mitte des Feldes beginnen wir mit dem Starken-Wettbewerb. Wir beginnen mit dem Gewichtheben. Danach präsentieren wir Hammerwurf und Baumstammweitwurf. 25 unserer stärksten schottischen Männer zeigen ihre Kräfte.
Die Namen der Sportler finden Sie ebenso im Programm wie die Regeln der verschiedenen Disziplinen. Es gibt 4 Schiedsrichter, die darauf achten, dass die Sportler sich an die Regeln halten. Wir hoffen, Sie genießen Ihren Aufenthalt in Braemar. Möge der Beste siegen.

C 5

Good afternoon, Ladies and Gentlemen!
Today is Saturday the 4th of September and I welcome you to our live-report about the Braemar Royal Highland Gathering. Referee Scott is sitting close to the field and waiting for the heavies.
(Some minutes later)
Now Aidan is tossing the caber – great – it looks as if he has scored the points!
On the other side of the field Conor is throwing the hammer.
(Some minutes later)
Now there are some funny games. The farmers are pulling the rope and showing their strength. On the other side of the field the teenagers are sack-racing.
Dancers from 6 to 18 years are showing their dances. Brian O'Neill is playing his bagpipes for them.
The local women at the refreshment stand are offering a lot of delicious meals today: You can have barbecued meat, hot dogs, corn on the cob, salads, sandwiches, home-made cakes and tea.
As it is almost every year the Queen is in Braemar, too. She is spending the summer holidays in Scotland – together with her Royal Family. Today they are joining the crowd at the Highland Games to show their interest in Scottish activities.

D 2

1. have, 2. have, 3. have, 4. have, 5. have, 6. has, 7. has, 8. have

ANSWER KEY

since: Easter, my last birthday, 1745, our last meeting, Christmas, the battle of Culloden, their wedding day
for: two weeks, centuries, five days, eight months, thirty minutes

D 3

No, Englishmen haven't always worn kilts.
No, the Mac Donalds haven't created a new kilt that looks like a pair of trousers.
No, the Scots haven't worn trousers for centuries.
No, I haven't seen a lot of men in kilts in Germany.
No, I haven't visited Bonnie Prince Charlie.
No, I haven't created a new pattern for the Mac Donalds.
Interview:
Have you ever worn a kilt?
Have you ever been to Scotland?
Have you ever visited a tartan store?
Have you ever seen the various clan patterns?
Have you ever heard about the 'Battle of Culloden'?
Have you ever read a book about the Highlanders?
Have you ever watched a film about Bonnie Prince Charlie?

D 4

Guten Tag, (womit) kann ich Ihnen helfen?
Ich würde gern einen Kilt anprobieren.
Haben Sie schon jemals einen Kilt getragen?
Nein, ich habe noch niemals vorher einen Kilt getragen. Ich habe bisher immer Hosen getragen.
Die Schotten haben den Kilt immer mit einer Tweedjacke, einem Gürtel, einem Sporran und einem Dolch getragen.
Ich habe gerade einen so bekleideten Mann bei den Highland Games gesehen.
Haben Sie Informationen über die Muster?
Ja, habe ich. Bis heute hat jeder Clan seinen eigenen, individuell gestalteten Kilt mit speziellen Farben und einem besonderen Muster. Diese Kilts werden aus einem Stoff namens „Tartan" gefertigt. In unserem Prospekt finden Sie einige der bekanntesten Clan-Muster.
Danke für diese interessanten Informationen. Jetzt möchte ich unbedingt einen Kilt als Souvenir kaufen.
Wie wäre es mit dem Kilt dort drüben – dem dunkelgrün-gelb gemusterten? Der würde Ihnen gut stehen.
... Ja, ich denke, den werde ich nehmen. Wie viel kostet er?

D 5

Introduction:
Members of the clan have always worn the big kilt. That's why McNally has decided to put on a big kilt for his visit to the Highland games.

a) McNally has put a belt on the floor.
b) He has placed the cloth on the belt.
c) He has measured the lower part of the cloth according to the length from waist to knee.
d) McNally has lain down on the cloth.
e) He has folded the cloth so that the edges overlap and he has closed the belt.
f) He has thrown the upper part of the cloth over the left shoulder.
g) He has fixed the cloth on the left shoulder with a brooch.
h) McNally has tucked the end of the cloth through the belt.

E 2

produce, produced, have/has produced
cause, caused, have/has caused
invent, invented, have/has invented
manufacture, manufactured, have/has manufactured
allow, allowed, have/has allowed
develop, developed, have/has developed
change, changed, have/has changed

make, made, have/has made
be, was/were, have/has been
give, gave, have/has given

E 3

John Napier didn't write a timetable (but) he wrote the logarithm tables.
Janet Keiller didn't preserve juice (but) she preserved marmalade.
James Bowman Lindsay didn't produce candle light (but) he produced continuous electric light.
James Dewar didn't develop the glass bottle (but) he developed the thermos flask.
John Dunlop didn't discover the wooden wheel (but) he discovered pneumatic tyres.
James Thomson didn't invent a heater (but) he invented a refrigerator.
James Watt didn't build a motor engine (but) he built a steam engine.
Kirkpatrick Macmillan didn't construct a motorbike (but) he constructed the pedal-powered bicycle.
James C. Maxwell didn't take a black and white photograph (but) he took the first colour photograph.
Alexander Graham Bell didn't communicate via the internet (but) he communicated by telephone.
Alexander Fleming didn't discover a cough mixture (but) he discovered penicillin.
John Logie Baird didn't produce a radio (but) he produced a television/TV.
Scientists at Roslin Institute didn't clone a goat (but) they cloned the sheep Dolly.

ANSWER KEY

E 5

The German baron Karl Friedrich Christian Ludwig Drais von Sauerbronn built a two-wheel bike.
He had to sit on the saddle and walk.
His invention was called "velocipede".
The velocipede helped people to move four times faster than on foot only.
This velocipede was used until 1839.
In 1939 Kirkpatrick Macmillan added two pedals that moved the back wheel.
This pedal-powered bicycle allowed people to move longer distances in a shorter time.
It became very popular.
That is why it was manufactured in large numbers.

F 2

First	Second
Example: had had breakfast	*left Inverness*
a. had organised	looked for
b. had arrived	visited
c. had noticed	went
d. had bought	went
e. had (already) left	got/arrived
f. had spoken	started
g. had seen	met
h. had heard	was interested in

F 3

1 They noticed something big swimming in the lake./They saw a strange head – bigger than a cow's head.
2 He had seen something with a long neck and a small head.
3 Because he was on holiday.
4 They started a project to find the monster.
5 They found that the water was very dark because of the peat./They couldn't see very far – so they didn't really find anything substantial.
6 They were frightened.
7 They saw a shadow of about six to nine metres in length.
8 They were very pleased. They used the story about "Nessie" in order to fill their hotels.
9 It was called "Nessie".
10 Because Loch Ness is very big and the water was very dark because of the peat.
11 Biological facts contradict the existence of a monster: mammals would need to surface regularly in order to breathe, beasts of prey couldn't find food in the Loch.
12 Because they thought it was a tourist attraction./ In order to show the photos of the eye witnesses and to collect all the other information.
13 Because it's the biggest of all Scottish lakes.
14 They believed that hotel managers invented Nessie ...
15 They didn't find anything.
16 Because he took four photos of "it".

F 4

a. Bei Nessie zu Hause

Mutter: Nessie-Baby, hast du den Fischen im Aquarium frisches Wasser gegeben, nachdem du sie gefüttert hattest?
Nessie: Nein Mama, sie hatten das Wasser vom letzten Mal noch nicht ausgetrunken.

b. Nessies Hobby: Motorboot fahren

Polizist: Nachdem du das Boot gestartet hattest, folgten wir dir. Du fuhrst 200 km die Stunde.
Nessie: Oh, ist doch toll. Ich habe erst gestern Motorboot fahren gelernt!

c. Freunde treffen

Nessie: Ich sah gestern einen Touristen, den ich seit 20 Jahren nicht gesehen hatte.
Sharky: Oh, das ist gar nichts. Ich habe gerade jemanden getroffen, den ich in meinem ganzen Leben noch nicht gesehen habe.

d. Vergessliche Nessie

Ducky: Nessie, hast du dein Bad gestern, nachdem du die Touristen erschreckt hattest, genossen?
Nessie: Nein, ich hatte vergessen, meine Kleider auszuziehen, bevor ich in die Wanne stieg.
Ducky: Oh, du Arme, bist du sehr nass geworden?
Nessie: Nein (war halb so wild), ich hatte vergessen, Wasser in die Wanne zu lassen!

F 5

Hello ...;
Greetings from Scotland. After we had made the GRAND TOUR and had visited a lot of castles we went to Loch Ness. As soon as we had arrived at Drumnadrochit we went to the Loch Ness Monster Exhibition. As you know, I don't believe that there is a monster. I had watched the photos of Nessie before I read the information about the scientific searches in the seventies.
The exhibition impressed me very much and after we had left I wasn't sure any longer if there is a monster or not.
Love, ...